This planner belongs to:

_____

Twenty-one

January

S	M	T	W	T	F	S
					1	2
3	4	5	6	7	8	9
10	11	12	13	14	15	16
17	18	19	20	21	22	23
24	25	26	27	28	29	30
31						

February

S	M	T	W	T	F	S
	1	2	3	4	5	6
7	8	9	10	11	12	13
14	15	16	17	18	19	20
21	22	23	24	25	26	27
28						

March

S	M	T	W	T	F	S
	1	2	3	4	5	6
7	8	9	10	11	12	13
14	15	16	17	18	19	20
21	22	23	24	25	26	27
28	29	30	31			

April

S	M	T	W	T	F	S
				1	2	3
4	5	6	7	8	9	10
11	12	13	14	15	16	17
18	19	20	21	22	23	24
25	26	27	28	29	30	

May

S	M	T	W	T	F	S
						1
2	3	4	5	6	7	8
9	10	11	12	13	14	15
16	17	18	19	20	21	22
23	24	25	26	27	28	29
30	31					

June

S	M	T	W	T	F	S
		1	2	3	4	5
6	7	8	9	10	11	12
13	14	15	16	17	18	19
20	21	22	23	24	25	26
27	28	29	30			

July

S	M	T	W	T	F	S
				1	2	3
4	5	6	7	8	9	10
11	12	13	14	15	16	17
18	19	20	21	22	23	24
25	26	27	28	29	30	31

August

S	M	T	W	T	F	S
1	2	3	4	5	6	7
8	9	10	11	12	13	14
15	16	17	18	19	20	21
22	23	24	25	26	27	28
29	30	31				

September

S	M	T	W	T	F	S
			1	2	3	4
5	6	7	8	9	10	11
12	13	14	15	16	17	18
19	20	21	22	23	24	25
26	27	28	29	30		

October

S	M	T	W	T	F	S
					1	2
3	4	5	6	7	8	9
10	11	12	13	14	15	16
17	18	19	20	21	22	23
24	25	26	27	28	29	30
31						

November

S	M	T	W	T	F	S
	1	2	3	4	5	6
7	8	9	10	11	12	13
14	15	16	17	18	19	20
21	22	23	24	25	26	27
28	29	30				

December

S	M	T	W	T	F	S
			1	2	3	4
5	6	7	8	9	10	11
12	13	14	15	16	17	18
19	20	21	22	23	24	25
26	27	28	29	30	31	

Year in Pixels

	J	F	M	A	M	J	J	A	S	O	N	D
1.												
2.												
3.												
4.												
5.												
6.												
7.												
8.												
9.												
10.												
11.												
12.												
13.												
14.												
15.												
16.												
17.												
18.												
19.												
20.												
21.												
22.												
23.												
24.												
25.												
26.												
27.												
28.												
29.												
30.												
31.												

Color Codes

Notes

January

SUNDAY	MONDAY	TUESDAY	WEDNESDAY
3	4	5	6
10	11	12	13
17	18	19	20
24	25	26	27

January

THURSDAY	FRIDAY	SATURDAY	NOTES
	1	2	○
			○
			○
			○
			○
7	8	9	○
			○
			○
			○
14	15	16	○
			○
			○
			○
			○
21	22	23	○
			○
			○
			○
			○
28	29	30	31

February

SUNDAY	MONDAY	TUESDAY	WEDNESDAY
	1	2	3
7	8	9	10
14	15	16	17
21	22	23	24
28			

February

2021

THURSDAY	FRIDAY	SATURDAY	NOTES
4	5	6	○
			○
			○
			○
			○
11	12	13	○
			○
			○
			○
18	19	20	○
			○
			○
			○
			○
25	26	27	○
			○
			○
			○
			○
			NOTES

March

SUNDAY	MONDAY	TUESDAY	WEDNESDAY
	1	2	3
7	8	9	10
14	15	16	17
21	22	23	24
28	29	30	31

March

THURSDAY	FRIDAY	SATURDAY	NOTES
4	5	6	○
			○
			○
			○
			○
11	12	13	○
			○
			○
			○
18	19	20	○
			○
			○
			○
			○
25	26	27	○
			○
			○
			○
			○
			NOTES

April

SUNDAY	MONDAY	TUESDAY	WEDNESDAY
4	5	6	7
11	12	13	14
18	19	20	21
25	26	27	28

April

2021

THURSDAY	FRIDAY	SATURDAY	NOTES
1	2	3	○
			○
			○
			○
			○
8	9	10	○
			○
			○
			○
15	16	17	○
			○
			○
			○
			○
22	23	24	○
			○
			○
			○
			○
29	30	1	NOTES

May

SUNDAY	MONDAY	TUESDAY	WEDNESDAY
2	3	4	5
9	10	11	12
16	17	18	19
23	24	25	26
30	31		

May

THURSDAY	FRIDAY	SATURDAY	NOTES
6	7	8	○
			○
			○
			○
			○
13	14	15	○
			○
			○
			○
20	21	22	○
			○
			○
			○
			○
27	28	29	○
			○
			○
			○
			○
			NOTES

June

SUNDAY	MONDAY	TUESDAY	WEDNESDAY
		1	2
6	7	8	9
13	14	15	16
20	21	22	23
27	28	29	30

June

2021

THURSDAY	FRIDAY	SATURDAY	NOTES
3	4	5	○
			○
			○
			○
			○
10	11	12	○
			○
			○
			○
17	18	19	○
			○
			○
			○
			○
24	25	26	○
			○
			○
			○
			○
			NOTES

July

SUNDAY	MONDAY	TUESDAY	WEDNESDAY
4	5	6	7
11	12	13	14
18	19	20	21
25	26	27	28

July

THURSDAY	FRIDAY	SATURDAY	NOTES
1	2	3	○
			○
			○
			○
			○
8	9	10	○
			○
			○
			○
15	16	17	○
			○
			○
			○
			○
22	23	24	○
			○
			○
			○
			○
29	30	31	NOTES

August

SUNDAY	MONDAY	TUESDAY	WEDNESDAY
1	2	3	4
8	9	10	11
15	16	17	18
22	23	24	25
29	30	31	

August

2021

THURSDAY	FRIDAY	SATURDAY	NOTES
5	6	7	○
			○
			○
			○
			○
12	13	14	○
			○
			○
			○
19	20	21	○
			○
			○
			○
			○
26	27	28	NOTES

September

SUNDAY	MONDAY	TUESDAY	WEDNESDAY
			1
5	6	7	8
12	13	14	15
19	20	21	22
26	27	28	29

September

THURSDAY	FRIDAY	SATURDAY	NOTES
2	3	4	○
			○
			○
			○
			○
9	10	11	○
			○
			○
			○
16	17	18	○
			○
			○
			○
			○
23	24	25	○
			○
			○
			○
			○
30			NOTES

October 2021

SUNDAY	MONDAY	TUESDAY	WEDNESDAY
3	4	5	6
10	11	12	13
17	18	19	20
24	25	26	27

October 2021

THURSDAY	FRIDAY	SATURDAY	NOTES
	1	2	○
			○
			○
			○
			○
7	8	9	○
			○
			○
			○
			○
14	15	16	○
			○
			○
			○
			○
21	22	23	○
			○
			○
			○
			○
28	29	30 / 31 SUNDAY	NOTES

November

2021

SUNDAY	MONDAY	TUESDAY	WEDNESDAY
	1	2	3
7	8	9	10
14	15	16	17
21	22	23	24
28	29	30	

November 2021

THURSDAY	FRIDAY	SATURDAY	NOTES
4	5	6	○
			○
			○
			○
			○
11	12	13	○
			○
			○
			○
			○
18	19	20	○
			○
			○
			○
			○
25	26	27	○
			○
			○
			○
			○
			NOTES

December

SUNDAY	MONDAY	TUESDAY	WEDNESDAY
			1
5	6	7	8
12	13	14	15
19	20	21	22
26	27	28	29

December 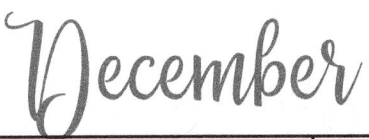 2021

THURSDAY	FRIDAY	SATURDAY	NOTES
2	3	4	○
			○
			○
			○
			○
9	10	11	○
			○
			○
			○
			○
16	17	18	○
			○
			○
			○
			○
23	24	25	○
			○
			○
			○
			○
30	31		NOTES

01 TUESDAY

○
○
○
○
○
○
○
○

02 WEDNESDAY

○
○
○
○
○
○
○
○

03 THURSDAY

○
○
○
○
○
○
○
○

04 FRIDAY

○
○
○
○
○

December
2020

05 SATURDAY

○
○
○
○
○
○
○
○

06 SUNDAY

○
○
○
○
○
○
○
○

07 MONDAY

○
○
○
○
○
○
○
○

08 TUESDAY

○
○
○
○
○

December
2020

09 WEDNESDAY

○
○
○
○
○
○
○
○

10 THURSDAY

○
○
○
○
○
○
○
○

11 FRIDAY

○
○
○
○
○
○
○
○

12 SATURDAY

○
○
○
○
○

13 SUNDAY

14 MONDAY

15 TUESDAY

16 WEDNESDAY

17 THURSDAY

18 FRIDAY

19 SATURDAY

20 SUNDAY

December
2020

21 MONDAY

○
○
○
○
○
○
○
○

22 TUESDAY

○
○
○
○
○
○
○
○

23 WEDNESDAY

○
○
○
○
○
○
○
○

24 THURSDAY

○
○
○
○
○

25 FRIDAY

○
○
○
○
○
○
○
○

26 SATURDAY

○
○
○
○
○
○
○
○

27 SUNDAY

○
○
○
○
○
○
○
○

28 MONDAY

○
○
○
○
○

December
2020

29 TUESDAY

○
○
○
○
○
○
○
○

30 WEDNESDAY

○
○
○
○
○
○
○
○

31 THURSDAY

○
○
○
○
○
○
○
○

NOTES

January
2021

01 FRIDAY

○ _____
○ _____
○ _____
○ _____
○ _____
○ _____
○ _____
○ _____

02 SATURDAY

○ _____
○ _____
○ _____
○ _____
○ _____
○ _____
○ _____
○ _____

03 SUNDAY

○ _____
○ _____
○ _____
○ _____
○ _____
○ _____
○ _____
○ _____

04 MONDAY

○ _____
○ _____
○ _____
○ _____
○ _____

05 TUESDAY

○ _____
○ _____
○ _____
○ _____
○ _____
○ _____
○ _____
○ _____

06 WEDNESDAY

○ _____
○ _____
○ _____
○ _____
○ _____
○ _____
○ _____
○ _____

07 THURSDAY

○ _____
○ _____
○ _____
○ _____
○ _____
○ _____
○ _____
○ _____

08 FRIDAY

○ _____
○ _____
○ _____
○ _____
○ _____

09 SATURDAY
- ○
- ○
- ○
- ○
- ○
- ○
- ○
- ○

10 SUNDAY
- ○
- ○
- ○
- ○
- ○
- ○
- ○
- ○

11 MONDAY
- ○
- ○
- ○
- ○
- ○
- ○
- ○
- ○

12 TUESDAY
- ○
- ○
- ○
- ○
- ○

13 WEDNESDAY

14 THURSDAY

15 FRIDAY

16 SATURDAY

17 SUNDAY

18 MONDAY

19 TUESDAY

20 WEDNESDAY

21 THURSDAY

22 FRIDAY

23 SATURDAY

24 SUNDAY

25 MONDAY

○
○
○
○
○
○
○
○

26 TUESDAY

○
○
○
○
○
○
○
○

27 WEDNESDAY

○
○
○
○
○
○
○
○

28 THURSDAY

○
○
○
○
○

29 FRIDAY

○ _____
○ _____
○ _____
○ _____
○ _____
○ _____
○ _____
○ _____

30 SATURDAY

○ _____
○ _____
○ _____
○ _____
○ _____
○ _____
○ _____
○ _____

31 SUNDAY

○ _____
○ _____
○ _____
○ _____
○ _____
○ _____
○ _____
○ _____

NOTES

_____
_____
_____
_____

01 MONDAY

○
○
○
○
○
○
○
○

02 TUESDAY

○
○
○
○
○
○
○
○

03 WEDNESDAY

○
○
○
○
○
○
○
○

04 THURSDAY

○
○
○
○
○

05 FRIDAY

○
○
○
○
○
○
○
○

06 SATURDAY

○
○
○
○
○
○
○
○

07 SUNDAY

○
○
○
○
○
○
○
○

08 MONDAY

○
○
○
○
○

09 TUESDAY

10 WEDNESDAY

11 THURSDAY

12 FRIDAY

13 SATURDAY

14 SUNDAY

15 MONDAY

16 TUESDAY

February 2021

17 WEDNESDAY
○
○
○
○
○
○
○
○

18 THURSDAY
○
○
○
○
○
○
○
○

19 FRIDAY
○
○
○
○
○
○
○
○

20 SATURDAY
○
○
○
○
○

February 2021

21 SUNDAY

○
○
○
○
○
○
○
○

22 MONDAY

○
○
○
○
○
○
○
○

23 TUESDAY

○
○
○
○
○
○
○
○

24 WEDNESDAY

○
○
○
○
○

February 2021

25 THURSDAY

○
○
○
○
○
○
○
○

26 FRIDAY

○
○
○
○
○
○
○
○

27 SATURDAY

○
○
○
○
○
○
○
○

28 SUNDAY

○
○
○
○
○

01 MONDAY
○
○
○
○
○
○
○
○

02 TUESDAY
○
○
○
○
○
○
○
○

03 WEDNESDAY
○
○
○
○
○
○
○
○

04 THURSDAY
○
○
○
○
○

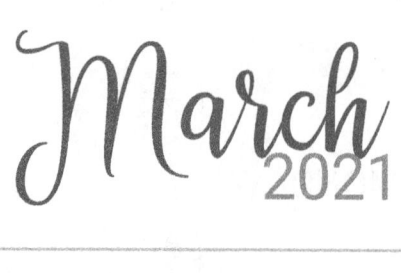

March
2021

05 FRIDAY

○
○
○
○
○
○
○
○

06 SATURDAY

○
○
○
○
○
○
○
○

07 SUNDAY

○
○
○
○
○
○
○
○

08 MONDAY

○
○
○
○
○

09 TUESDAY

10 WEDNESDAY

11 THURSDAY

12 FRIDAY

13 SATURDAY

○
○
○
○
○
○
○
○

14 SUNDAY

○
○
○
○
○
○
○
○

15 MONDAY

○
○
○
○
○
○
○
○

16 TUESDAY

○
○
○
○
○

17 WEDNESDAY

18 THURSDAY

19 FRIDAY

20 SATURDAY

21 SUNDAY

22 MONDAY

23 TUESDAY

24 WEDNESDAY

25 THURSDAY

○
○
○
○
○
○
○
○

26 FRIDAY

○
○
○
○
○
○
○
○

27 SATURDAY

○
○
○
○
○
○
○
○

28 SUNDAY

○
○
○
○
○

29 MONDAY

○
○
○
○
○
○
○
○

30 TUESDAY

○
○
○
○
○
○
○
○

31 WEDNESDAY

○
○
○
○
○
○
○
○

NOTES

01 THURSDAY

02 FRIDAY

03 SATURDAY

04 SUNDAY

April
2021

05 MONDAY

06 TUESDAY

07 WEDNESDAY

08 THURSDAY

09 FRIDAY

○
○
○
○
○
○
○

10 SATURDAY

○
○
○
○
○
○
○
○

11 SUNDAY

○
○
○
○
○
○
○
○

12 MONDAY

○
○
○
○
○

13 TUESDAY

14 WEDNESDAY

15 THURSDAY

16 FRIDAY

17 SATURDAY

18 SUNDAY

19 MONDAY

20 TUESDAY

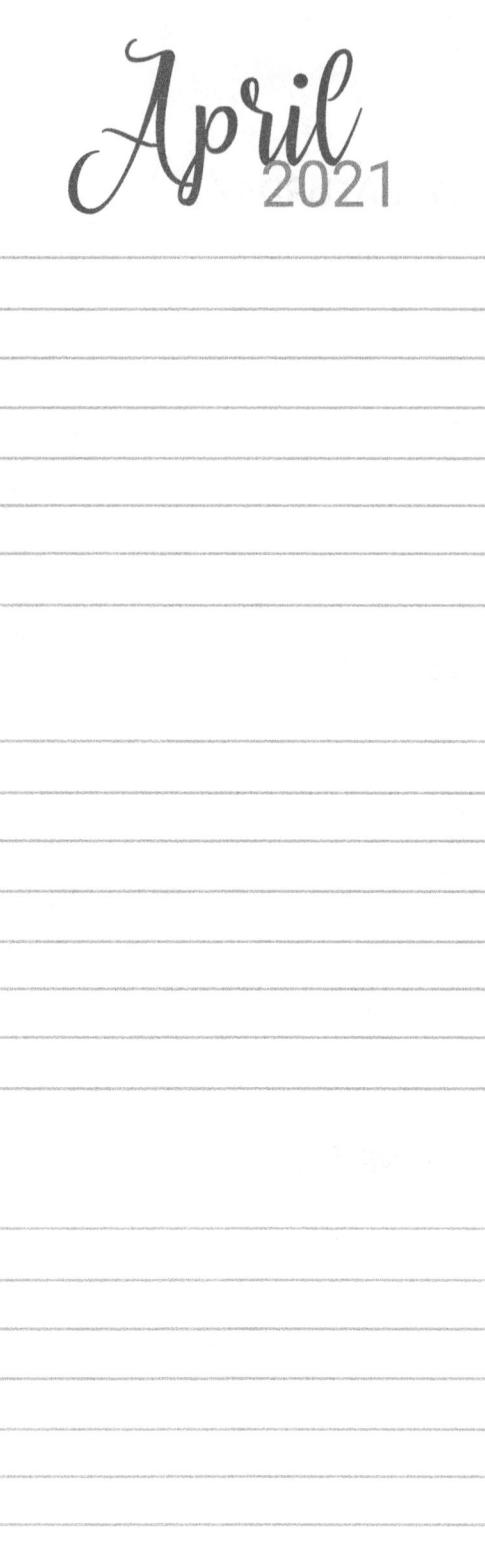

21 WEDNESDAY

○
○
○
○
○
○
○
○

22 THURSDAY

○
○
○
○
○
○
○
○

23 FRIDAY

○
○
○
○
○
○
○
○

24 SATURDAY

○
○
○
○
○

April
2021

25 SUNDAY

○
○
○
○
○
○
○

26 MONDAY

○
○
○
○
○
○
○
○

27 TUESDAY

○
○
○
○
○
○
○
○

28 WEDNESDAY

○
○
○
○
○

April
2021

29 THURSDAY

○
○
○
○
○
○
○
○

30 FRIDAY

○
○
○
○
○
○
○
○

NOTES

May
2021

01 SATURDAY

○
○
○
○
○
○
○
○

02 SUNDAY

○
○
○
○
○
○
○
○

03 MONDAY

○
○
○
○
○
○
○
○

04 TUESDAY

○
○
○
○
○

May
2021

05 WEDNESDAY

06 THURSDAY

07 FRIDAY

08 SATURDAY

May
2021

09 SUNDAY

○
○
○
○
○
○
○
○

10 MONDAY

○
○
○
○
○
○
○
○

11 TUESDAY

○
○
○
○
○
○
○
○

12 WEDNESDAY

○
○
○
○
○

13 THURSDAY

○
○
○
○
○
○
○
○

14 FRIDAY

○
○
○
○
○
○
○
○

15 SATURDAY

○
○
○
○
○
○
○
○

16 SUNDAY

○
○
○
○
○

May
2021

17 MONDAY

○
○
○
○
○
○
○
○

18 TUESDAY

○
○
○
○
○
○
○
○

19 WEDNESDAY

○
○
○
○
○
○
○
○

20 THURSDAY

○
○
○
○
○

21 FRIDAY

○
○ _____
○ _____
○ _____
○ _____
○ _____
○ _____

22 SATURDAY

○
○ _____
○ _____
○ _____
○ _____
○ _____
○ _____
○ _____

23 SUNDAY

○
○ _____
○ _____
○ _____
○ _____
○ _____
○ _____
○ _____

24 MONDAY

○
○ _____
○ _____
○ _____
○ _____

May
2021

25 TUESDAY
○
○
○
○
○
○
○
○

26 WEDNESDAY
○
○
○
○
○
○
○
○

27 THURSDAY
○
○
○
○
○
○
○
○

28 FRIDAY
○
○
○
○
○

May
2021

29 SATURDAY

- ○
- ○
- ○
- ○
- ○
- ○
- ○
- ○

30 SUNDAY

- ○
- ○
- ○
- ○
- ○
- ○
- ○
- ○

31 MONDAY

- ○
- ○
- ○
- ○
- ○
- ○
- ○
- ○

NOTES

01 TUESDAY

○
○
○
○
○
○
○
○

02 WEDNESDAY

○
○
○
○
○
○
○
○

03 THURSDAY

○
○
○
○
○
○
○
○

04 FRIDAY

○
○
○
○

June
2021

05 SATURDAY

○ _____
○ _____
○ _____
○ _____
○ _____
○ _____
○ _____
○ _____

06 SUNDAY

○ _____
○ _____
○ _____
○ _____
○ _____
○ _____
○ _____
○ _____

07 MONDAY

○ _____
○ _____
○ _____
○ _____
○ _____
○ _____
○ _____
○ _____

08 TUESDAY

○ _____
○ _____
○ _____
○ _____
○ _____

09 WEDNESDAY

- ○
- ○
- ○
- ○
- ○
- ○
- ○
- ○

10 THURSDAY

- ○
- ○
- ○
- ○
- ○
- ○
- ○
- ○

11 FRIDAY

- ○
- ○
- ○
- ○
- ○
- ○
- ○
- ○

12 SATURDAY

- ○
- ○
- ○
- ○
- ○

13 SUNDAY

○
○
○
○
○
○
○
○

14 MONDAY

○
○
○
○
○
○
○
○
○

15 TUESDAY

○
○
○
○
○
○
○
○

16 WEDNESDAY

○
○
○
○
○

17 THURSDAY

○
○
○
○
○
○
○
○

18 FRIDAY

○
○
○
○
○
○
○
○
○

19 SATURDAY

○
○
○
○
○
○
○
○
○

20 SUNDAY

○
○
○
○
○

21 MONDAY

○
○
○
○
○
○
○
○

22 TUESDAY

○
○
○
○
○
○
○
○

23 WEDNESDAY

○
○
○
○
○
○
○
○

24 THURSDAY

○
○
○
○
○

25 FRIDAY
○
○
○
○
○
○
○
○

26 SATURDAY
○
○
○
○
○
○
○
○

27 SUNDAY
○
○
○
○
○
○
○
○

28 MONDAY
○
○
○
○
○

29 TUESDAY

- ○ _____
- ○ _____
- ○ _____
- ○ _____
- ○ _____
- ○ _____
- ○ _____
- ○ _____

30 WEDNESDAY

- ○ _____
- ○ _____
- ○ _____
- ○ _____
- ○ _____
- ○ _____
- ○ _____
- ○ _____

NOTES

July
2021

01 THURSDAY
- ○
- ○
- ○
- ○
- ○
- ○
- ○
- ○

02 FRIDAY
- ○
- ○
- ○
- ○
- ○
- ○
- ○
- ○

03 SATURDAY
- ○
- ○
- ○
- ○
- ○
- ○
- ○
- ○

04 SUNDAY
- ○
- ○
- ○
- ○
- ○

July
2021

05 MONDAY

○
○
○
○
○
○
○
○

06 TUESDAY

○
○
○
○
○
○
○
○

07 WEDNESDAY

○
○
○
○
○
○
○
○

08 THURSDAY

○
○
○
○
○

09 FRIDAY

○
○
○
○
○
○
○
○

10 SATURDAY

○
○
○
○
○
○
○
○
○

11 SUNDAY

○
○
○
○
○
○
○
○

12 MONDAY

○
○
○
○
○

13 TUESDAY

○
○
○
○
○
○
○
○

14 WEDNESDAY

○
○
○
○
○
○
○
○

15 THURSDAY

○
○
○
○
○
○
○
○

16 FRIDAY

○
○
○
○
○

17 SATURDAY
○
○
○
○
○
○
○
○

18 SUNDAY
○
○
○
○
○
○
○
○

19 MONDAY
○
○
○
○
○
○
○
○

20 TUESDAY
○
○
○
○
○

21 WEDNESDAY
○
○
○
○
○
○
○
○

22 THURSDAY
○
○
○
○
○
○
○
○

23 FRIDAY
○
○
○
○
○
○
○
○

24 SATURDAY
○
○
○
○
○

July

25 SUNDAY

○
○
○
○
○
○
○

26 MONDAY

○
○
○
○
○
○
○
○
○

27 TUESDAY

○
○
○
○
○
○
○
○

28 WEDNESDAY

○
○
○
○
○

July
2021

29 THURSDAY

30 FRIDAY

31 SATURDAY

NOTES

August
2021

01 SUNDAY

○
○
○
○
○
○
○
○

02 MONDAY

○
○
○
○
○
○
○
○

03 TUESDAY

○
○
○
○
○
○
○
○

04 WEDNESDAY

○
○
○
○
○

August
2021

05 THURSDAY

○
○
○
○
○
○
○
○

06 FRIDAY

○
○
○
○
○
○
○
○

07 SATURDAY

○
○
○
○
○
○
○
○

08 SUNDAY

○
○
○
○
○

August
2021

09 MONDAY
○
○
○
○
○
○
○
○

10 TUESDAY
○
○
○
○
○
○
○
○
○

11 WEDNESDAY
○
○
○
○
○
○
○
○
○

12 THURSDAY
○
○
○
○
○

13 FRIDAY

○
○
○
○
○
○
○
○

14 SATURDAY

○
○
○
○
○
○
○
○

15 SUNDAY

○
○
○
○
○
○
○
○

16 MONDAY

○
○
○
○
○

August
2021

17 TUESDAY

○
○
○
○
○
○
○
○

18 WEDNESDAY

○
○
○
○
○
○
○
○

19 THURSDAY

○
○
○
○
○
○
○
○

20 FRIDAY

○
○
○
○
○

21 SATURDAY

○ _____
○ _____
○ _____
○ _____
○ _____
○ _____
○ _____
○ _____

22 SUNDAY

○ _____
○ _____
○ _____
○ _____
○ _____
○ _____
○ _____
○ _____

23 MONDAY

○ _____
○ _____
○ _____
○ _____
○ _____
○ _____
○ _____
○ _____

24 TUESDAY

○ _____
○ _____
○ _____
○ _____
○ _____

25 WEDNESDAY

○
○
○
○
○
○
○
○

26 THURSDAY

○
○
○
○
○
○
○
○

27 FRIDAY

○
○
○
○
○
○
○
○

28 SATURDAY

○
○
○
○
○

August
2021

29 SUNDAY

30 MONDAY

31 TUESDAY

NOTES

September
2021

01 WEDNESDAY

○ _____
○ _____
○ _____
○ _____
○ _____
○ _____
○ _____
○ _____

02 THURSDAY

○ _____
○ _____
○ _____
○ _____
○ _____
○ _____
○ _____
○ _____

03 FRIDAY

○ _____
○ _____
○ _____
○ _____
○ _____
○ _____
○ _____
○ _____

04 SATURDAY

○ _____
○ _____
○ _____
○ _____
○ _____

05 SUNDAY

○ _____
○ _____
○ _____
○ _____
○ _____
○ _____
○ _____
○ _____

06 MONDAY

○ _____
○ _____
○ _____
○ _____
○ _____
○ _____
○ _____
○ _____

07 TUESDAY

○ _____
○ _____
○ _____
○ _____
○ _____
○ _____
○ _____
○ _____

08 WEDNESDAY

○ _____
○ _____
○ _____
○ _____
○ _____

09 THURSDAY

○
○
○
○
○
○
○
○

10 FRIDAY

○
○
○
○
○
○
○
○

11 SATURDAY

○
○
○
○
○
○
○
○

12 SUNDAY

○
○
○
○
○

13 MONDAY

○
○
○
○
○
○
○
○

14 TUESDAY

○
○
○
○
○
○
○
○

15 WEDNESDAY

○
○
○
○
○
○
○
○

16 THURSDAY

○
○
○
○
○

17 FRIDAY

○
○
○
○
○
○
○
○

18 SATURDAY

○
○
○
○
○
○
○
○

19 SUNDAY

○
○
○
○
○
○
○
○

20 MONDAY

○
○
○
○
○

21 TUESDAY

22 WEDNESDAY

23 THURSDAY

24 FRIDAY

25 SATURDAY

○
○
○
○
○
○
○
○

26 SUNDAY

○
○
○
○
○
○
○
○

27 MONDAY

○
○
○
○
○
○
○
○

28 TUESDAY

○
○
○
○
○

29 WEDNESDAY

- ○
- ○
- ○
- ○
- ○
- ○
- ○
- ○

30 THURSDAY

- ○
- ○
- ○
- ○
- ○
- ○
- ○
- ○

NOTES

October
2021

01 FRIDAY

○
○
○
○
○
○
○
○

02 SATURDAY

○
○
○
○
○
○
○
○

03 SUNDAY

○
○
○
○
○
○
○
○

04 MONDAY

○
○
○
○
○

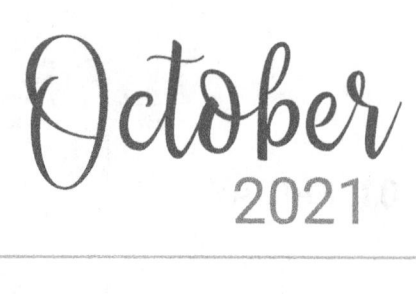

October
2021

05 TUESDAY

○ _____
○ _____
○ _____
○ _____
○ _____
○ _____
○ _____
○ _____

06 WEDNESDAY

○ _____
○ _____
○ _____
○ _____
○ _____
○ _____
○ _____
○ _____

07 THURSDAY

○ _____
○ _____
○ _____
○ _____
○ _____
○ _____
○ _____
○ _____

08 FRIDAY

○ _____
○ _____
○ _____
○ _____
○ _____

October
2021

09 SATURDAY

○
○
○
○
○
○
○
○

10 SUNDAY

○
○
○
○
○
○
○
○

11 MONDAY

○
○
○
○
○
○
○
○

12 TUESDAY

○
○
○
○
○

13 WEDNESDAY

14 THURSDAY

15 FRIDAY

16 SATURDAY

October
2021

17 SUNDAY

18 MONDAY

19 TUESDAY

20 WEDNESDAY

October
2021

21 THURSDAY

○
○
○
○
○
○
○
○

22 FRIDAY

○
○
○
○
○
○
○
○

23 SATURDAY

○
○
○
○
○
○
○
○

24 SUNDAY

○
○
○
○
○

October
2021

25 MONDAY

○
○
○
○
○
○
○
○

26 TUESDAY

○
○
○
○
○
○
○
○

27 WEDNESDAY

○
○
○
○
○
○
○
○

28 THURSDAY

○
○
○
○
○

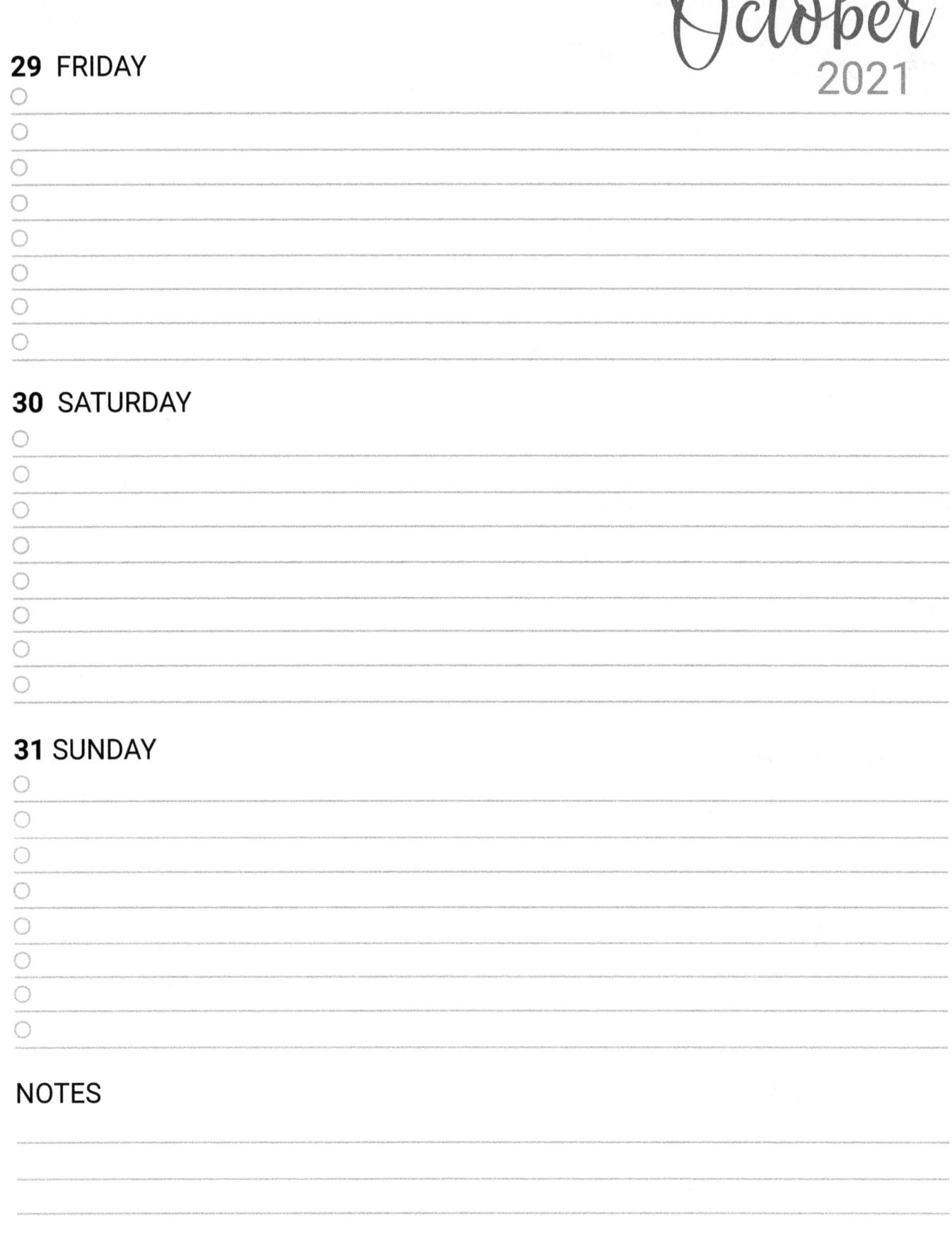

October
2021

29 FRIDAY

○
○
○
○
○
○
○
○

30 SATURDAY

○
○
○
○
○
○
○
○

31 SUNDAY

○
○
○
○
○
○
○
○

NOTES

01 MONDAY

02 TUESDAY

03 WEDNESDAY

04 THURSDAY

05 FRIDAY

06 SATURDAY

07 SUNDAY

08 MONDAY

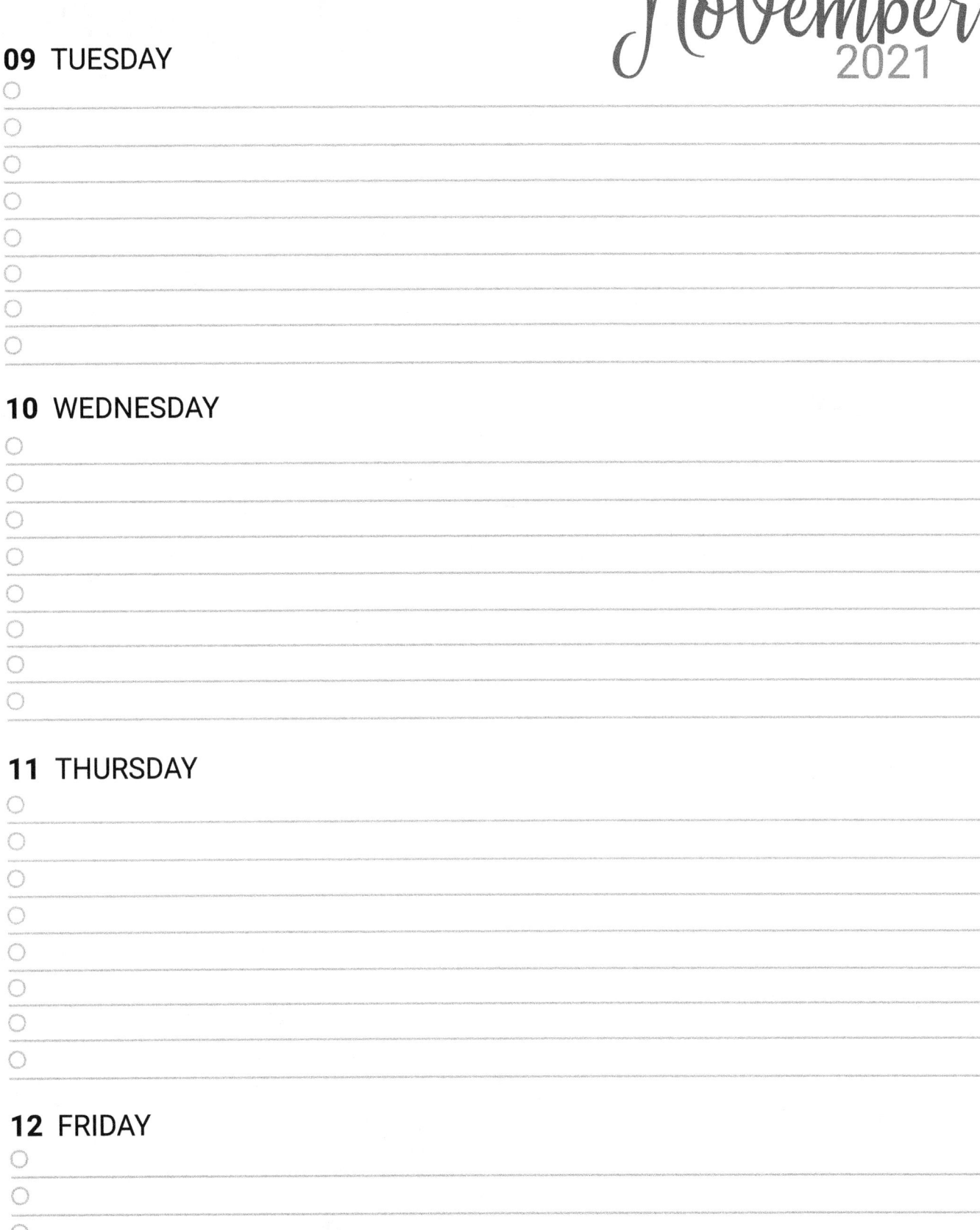

November
2021

09 TUESDAY

10 WEDNESDAY

11 THURSDAY

12 FRIDAY

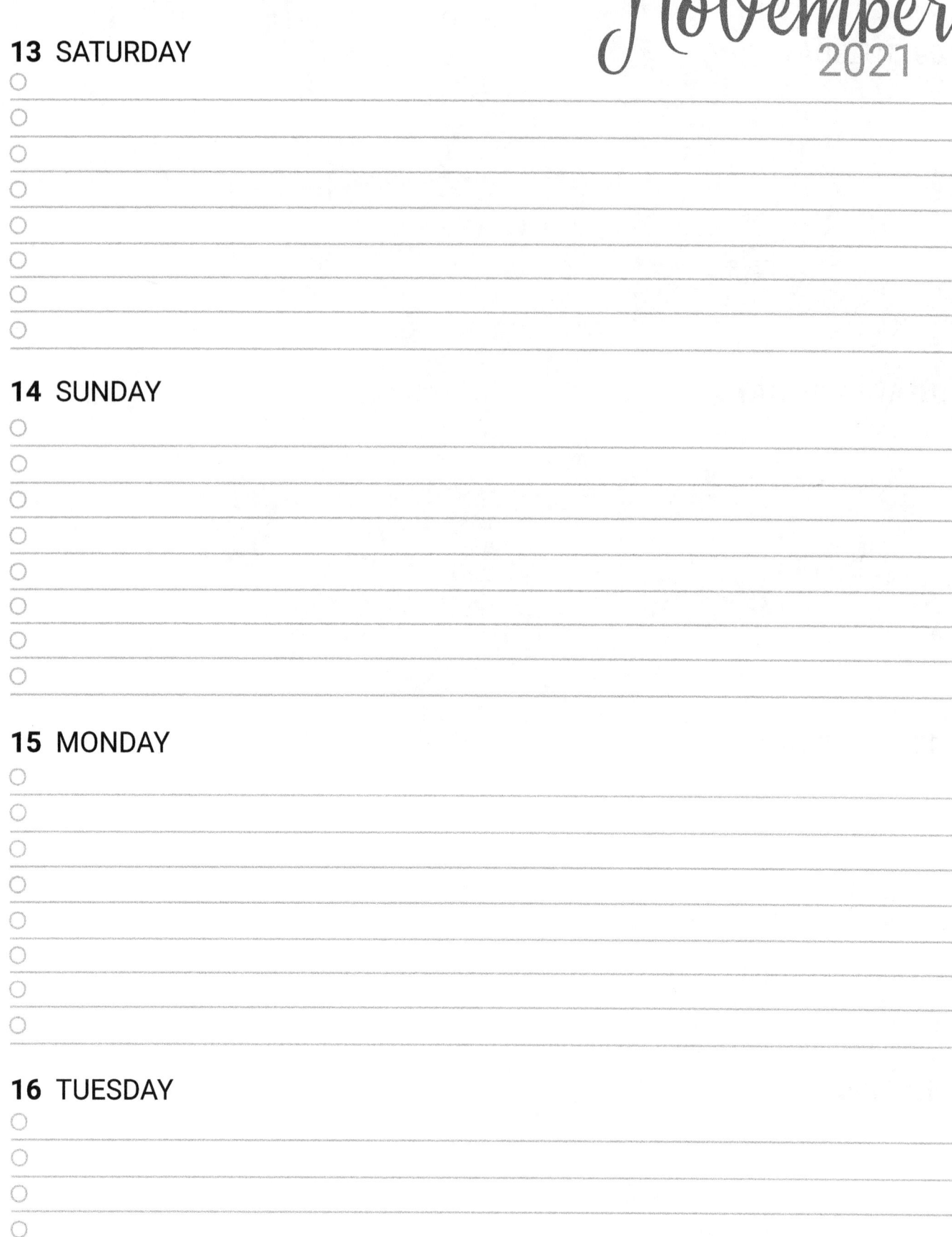

November
2021

13 SATURDAY

○
○
○
○
○
○
○
○

14 SUNDAY

○
○
○
○
○
○
○
○

15 MONDAY

○
○
○
○
○
○
○
○

16 TUESDAY

○
○
○
○
○

17 WEDNESDAY

18 THURSDAY

19 FRIDAY

20 SATURDAY

November
2021

21 SUNDAY

22 MONDAY

23 TUESDAY

24 WEDNESDAY

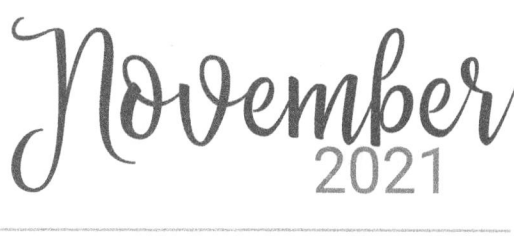

November
2021

25 THURSDAY

○
○
○
○
○
○
○
○

26 FRIDAY

○
○
○
○
○
○
○
○

27 SATURDAY

○
○
○
○
○
○
○
○

28 SUNDAY

○
○
○
○
○

29 MONDAY

- ○ _____
- ○ _____
- ○ _____
- ○ _____
- ○ _____
- ○ _____
- ○ _____
- ○ _____

30 TUESDAY

- ○ _____
- ○ _____
- ○ _____
- ○ _____
- ○ _____
- ○ _____
- ○ _____
- ○ _____

NOTES

01 WEDNESDAY

-
-
-
-
-
-
-
-

02 THURSDAY

-
-
-
-
-
-
-
-

03 FRIDAY

-
-
-
-
-
-
-
-

04 SATURDAY

-
-
-
-
-

December
2021

05 SUNDAY
○
○
○
○
○
○
○
○

06 MONDAY
○
○
○
○
○
○
○
○

07 TUESDAY
○
○
○
○
○
○
○
○

08 WEDNESDAY
○
○
○
○
○

December
2021

09 THURSDAY

10 FRIDAY

11 SATURDAY

12 SUNDAY

December
2021

13 MONDAY

○
○
○
○
○
○
○
○

14 TUESDAY

○
○
○
○
○
○
○
○

15 WEDNESDAY

○
○
○
○
○
○
○
○

16 THURSDAY

○
○
○
○
○

December
2021

17 FRIDAY

○
○
○
○
○
○
○
○

18 SATURDAY

○
○
○
○
○
○
○
○
○

19 SUNDAY

○
○
○
○
○
○
○
○

20 MONDAY

○
○
○
○
○

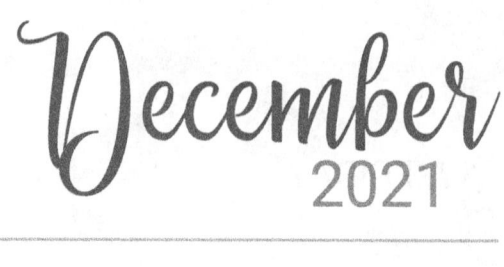
December
2021

21 TUESDAY

○
○
○
○
○
○
○
○

22 WEDNESDAY

○
○
○
○
○
○
○
○

23 THURSDAY

○
○
○
○
○
○
○
○

24 FRIDAY

○
○
○
○
○

December
2021

25 SATURDAY

○
○
○
○
○
○
○
○

26 SUNDAY

○
○
○
○
○
○
○
○

27 MONDAY

○
○
○
○
○
○
○
○

28 TUESDAY

○
○
○
○
○

29 WEDNESDAY

30 THURSDAY

31 FRIDAY

NOTES